The Pro's Playbook

A Benchwarmer's Success Story

by

Laurick Ingram

Author's Page

Your time is a precious gift. Reading this means you are sharing part of that gift with me. Thank you.

I want to thank Irving Thomas, retired NBA player and current Head Talent Scout for the Los Angeles Lakers. This book grew out of our 40-plus-year friendship. One of the greatest lessons our friendship taught us is whether you are basketball player or a bricklayer, do it like a pro.

Copyright © 2018 Laurick Ingram
All rights reserved.

Preface

Growing up, I sucked at sports. The only team I made it on was in the seventh grade. The team was the Holy Redeemer Hawks, or maybe it was the Falcons; one of those big birds. I was a third string guard, a position I think Coach Coleman created to make space on the team for benchwarmers like me. The team's uniform was gold with navy blue lettering. My number was 00.

Most of my nonplaying time was spent on the sidelines terrified that Coach Coleman would say, "Laurick you're in!" Then not only the teams, but the spectators would see just how bad I was. After an entire season of nail biting, stomach churning dread, I was put in with a minute left in the last game of the season. For some bizarre reason, the ball was inbounded to me and my teammates were screaming "Shoot! "Shoot!" I shot. I missed. That marked the inauspicious end of my school playing career.

Given the low point of my athletic performance, you would think it could not get worse, but it could and did. I failed physical education—that's right P.E.—in the 10th grade at Miami Springs High, another school with a bird for a mascot. I should have caught the hint that big birds hated me. With a backstory like that, what could I possibly know about doing anything like a pro. What I know is change is possible to those who believe, and failure is only final to those who gave up.

My change began near the end of the 10th grade. My older brother Kelsey, his friends called him "Chick," came over to the house. My mom and dad had 11 children. Chick was the fourth and I was the eleventh and there was 12 years between us. In our mom's living room, he asked me to drop down and do ten pushups. I strained through eight before collapsing on the wooden floor. He asked me to walk to his car with him. He popped the trunk and inside was a 110-pound set of Weider dumbbells. He told me to start doing pushups every day and showed me what he called the basic six exercises: bench presses, squats, biceps curls, triceps curls, overhead presses, and bent over rows. I was to do four sets of ten reps of each exercise three days a week. Every few weeks I was to increase the weight by five or ten pounds until I reached my limit. Because I failed P.E., I had to go to summer school. I transferred from Miami Springs to Miami Central where I took four hours of P.E. and one hour of English. The sport *du jour* for summer school was volleyball, which surprisingly I was good at. I nailed four A's that summer and also got at A in English, another class I had failed a Miami Springs.

I began my eleventh-grade year as a Miami Central Rocket—thank God their mascot wasn't a bird—where the school motto is *ad astra per aspera* (through hardships to the stars). By the end of the eleventh grade, could do 50 pushups, bench press the entire Universal rack (275 pounds), and had packed on thirty pounds of muscle mass. One day in Beck's Barbershop, I bumped into Coach Rolle. He coached Miami Central High's football team.

I said, "Hello Coach."

He squinted and asked, "You know me?"

"Yes," I said, "I go to Central."

"You don't play ball?" He asked.

"No sir."

"I tell you what," he said, "if you come out for the team, I guarantee I will start you at linebacker."

"No, sir," was my answer. What he did not know was that despite my outer appearance, the inner benchwarmer still lurked in my heart. Maybe I would have made the team or maybe I would not have. I will never know because I never tried, and you miss 100% of the shots you don't take.

I did continue my weight training and running. Ten years later, when I entered the police academy, I was in such good shape that I finished first place in my class in physical fitness. The regime included an obstacle course, swimming, running, pushups, pullups, sit ups, and defensive tactics. One way the police academy differed from my school days was that by then, Irv and I had been friends for six years. Although I was seven years older than he was, watching him, I learned what it took to be a pro. Also, I realized the skills it took to be a pro worked on and off the courts. The same skills that fueled his journey from Lake Stevens Middle School to the Los Angeles Lakers, propelled me from pumping gas to police officer of the year. I went from a terrified benchwarmer to a winning a medal of valor for bravery. All because I learned that if you look like a pro, swim like a pro, and quack like a pro, you can live life like a pro.

* * *

Is this book for you? It depends. If you were the head coach over your team, would you consider yourself one of your team's most valuable players? If you were the author (and by the way you are whether you know it or not) writing the story of your life, would you be one of the heroes of your story? If the answer to those questions is yes, this book will probably re-enforce many things you already know. If the answer is no, this book will show you how to prepare your body, soul, heart, and mind to elevate yourself to superstar status in whatever field you choose. This book is not only for athletes, because you can live life like a pro no matter your chosen field or avocation.

The American military is a good example of this. In the military, only a small percentage of the soldiers see combat. The remainder support them with everything from food, housing, clothing, transportation, communication, and medical care.

It takes diverse organs and cells to make up the human body. It takes bankers, business owners, caregivers, coaches, cooks, doctors, first responders, housekeepers, lawyers, managers, parents, pilots, salespeople, teachers, and writers to make a pro. In life, it is up to you to choose what game in life you will play and where you will play it. Whatever your choice, commit right now to do it like a pro.

We believe anyone can live like a pro, no matter where they are and what they have. My brother Kelsey used to tell me a story about Big J. and Little J., walking through the forest. One day

Little J. says to Big J., "If I were as big as you, I would find me a great big bear and wrestle him to the ground." Big J. looked down at Little J. and said, "There are plenty of small bears in the forest." The moral of the story is to do whatever you can, with what you have, where you are.

In the forest of life, Lebron James lives life like a pro in the area of professional basketball, and even non-basketball aficionados can cite many of his achievements on and off the court. From winning championships, to launching a school, creating his own clothing lines, getting, or securing endorsement contracts. Millions of people know the name Lebron James. Fewer people know the name Jeanne Lewis Albaugh. She is a pro in the area of homeless awareness. For years, Jeanne was homeless and lived under a bridge in Davie, Florida. Today, she is the CEO of Showering with Love, a non-profit organization founded by her. Her team converted a bus they named Grace into a mobile shower station. They go out to places where the homeless are living and allow them to take showers, then give them care packages of clean clothes and other necessities. At the time of this writing, more than 2,000 of South Florida's homeless people have scrubbed, showered, and shaved on Grace. What makes James and Jeanne pros is that their actions make real the spirit of Douglas Malloch's poem: "Be the Best of Whatever You Are."

If you can't be a pine on the top of the hill,

Be a scrub in the valley—but be
The best little scrub by the side of the rill;
Be a bush if you can't be a tree.

If you can't be a bush be a bit of the grass,
And some highway happier make;
If you can't be a muskie then just be a bass—
But the liveliest bass in the lake!

We can't all be captains, we've got to be crew,
There's something for all of us here,
There's big work to do, and there's lesser to do,
And the task you must do is the near.

If you can't be a highway then just be a trail,
If you can't be the sun be a star;
It isn't by size that you win, or you fail—
Be the best of whatever you are!

Whether you are Big J. or Little J., you can live life like a pro, and we are going to show you how.

Let's get started!

Table of Contents

Introduction: The pro thinks, "What if this does work?"

Chapter 1: The pro quickly changes strategies and tactics in response to real-time results.

Chapter 2: The pro works and plays inside the temple of his or her desire.

Chapter 3: The pro has faith with wisdom.

Chapter 4: The pro asks, "What can we do for each other?"

Chapter 5: The pro is willing to launch.

Chapter 6: The pro is propelled by failure.

Chapter 7: The pro focuses on the present solutions.

Chapter 8: The pro seeks criticism and feedback.

Chapter 9: The pro asks what needs doing.

Chapter 10: The pro starts before time.

Chapter 11: The pro under promises and over

delivers.

Chapter 12: The pro can admit being wrong.

Chapter 13: The pro thinks action is more important than ambition.

Chapter 14: The pro faces fear.

Chapter 15: The pro says, "I'm hurting, but I can play."

Chapter 16: The pro says, "I practice even when I don't feel like it."

Chapter 17: The pro believes it matters whether I win or lose, and how I play the game.

Chapter 18: The pro has the audacity to believe in the unseen.

Chapter 19: The pro faults self when something is not working.

Chapter 20: The pro wants to be coached.

Chapter 21: The pro pivots when something is not working.

Chapter 22: The pro failed six times but succeeded the seventh time.

Chapter 23: The pro acts based on vision.

Chapter 24: The pro falls going forward.

Chapter 25: The pro learns from past mistakes.

Chapter 26: The pro knows how to use tools of opportunity.

Chapter 27: The pro knows the difference in having a best friend and being best friends.

Afterword

Acknowledgments

About the Author

Introduction

The pro thinks, "What if this does work?"

Henry Ford said, "Whether you think you can or whether you think you can't, you're right." Many people approach a new task believing it will not work or they cannot do it. Surprise, surprise, it often does not work, and they often do not do it. Playing or performing at a higher level than the one you are currently performing at requires you to be a *possibility thinker*. If you approach this book and the suggestions herein with a mindset of, "It is possible, it can work, and I can do it," ways that it can work, and you can do it will come to you. Conversely, if you approach it with the mindset of, "It is not possible it can't work and I can't do it," you will find ways that it can't work, and you can't do it. For the time you spend with us we want you to suspend your disbelief that you cannot do what we suggest. To quote Thomas Jefferson, "If you want something you never had, you must be willing to do something you have never done." If you are not, but want to be a professional author, basketball player, chef, doctor, event planner, fisherman, goalie, hang glider, inventor, jazz pianist, lover, musician, novelist, ophthalmologist, pilot, quilter, soldier, teacher, university scholar,

Laurick Ingram

videographer, writer, xylophone player, yodeler, or zoologist . . . you will have to do some things you have never done before.

Action Step

↑ Pick a task that will take no more than one day to one week to complete. It can be changing a light bulb. Approach it, giving three good reasons why it will not work, and then prove to yourself that it will not work by making sure those things happen. Then approach the same task with a can-do attitude and find ways to work around the three good reasons it did not work. Pay close attention to the words you use to describe both, and how you feel when planning and doing either. Use this strategy to see what situations in life you are looking at through a "can't-do" lens, versus a "can-do" lens.

Chapter 1

The pro quickly changes strategies and tactics in response to real-time results.

Laurick sharing: When I was nineteen and had decided to drop out of college, I talked it over with my brother Ronald. I explained to him that I did not think I needed college because "I had a lot of potential." Ronald said, "The problem is that often potential remains just that, the potential to do something, not actually doing it." One of the flaws in my thinking was that I was making decisions based on what I thought I could do, not what I was doing. In my mind, I thought I could do something great, even though I had no idea what that something great was. At that time, other than getting my college education, I was working as a cashier in a Quik Mart. I would like to tell you that I listened to my brother and stayed in college, but I did not. I continued at Quik Mart, and the potential to do something great was just that, the potential to do something great, without ever doing it.

A year later, I was at the Miami International Airport and bumped into a college professor that knew me. I happened to be wearing my red Quik Mart polo shirt. He smiled and said, "Get back in school." I did, and I graduated.

I do not think college is for everyone; each

person must decide for his or herself. I do believe in the absence of a clear, pressing, and precise plan that staying in an environment like college that trains, teaches, and challenges you is the better alternative.

Whether the year it took me to return to college was a quick or slow change to the real-time results of my life is relative to the arc of life I have lived. I did, however, change my strategies and tactics in response to real-time results.

Action Step

↑ Pick an area of your life where you see yourself doing great in your mind. Challenge yourself to measure your actual success objectively. If you cannot measure it objectively, nor can you find others you trust to agree you are as good as you think you are, change your tactics and strategies.

Chapter 2

The pro works and plays inside the temple of his or her desire.

The temple of your desire is the physical, mental, emotional, and spiritual space in which the thing or things you want exist.

When Irv was in the ninth grade, he heard about a team comprised of the best high school basketball players in Florida. The team was a summer league that practiced on Saturdays. Irv wanted to be on that team and believed that he could be one of the best high school players in Florida. He caught a bus to Miami-Dade College's North Campus where he saw the players practicing. At that time, he did not know what was required to be on the team; he only knew whatever was required, he was willing to do it. That year the team was already chosen, but he showed up every Saturday and played pickup games on the side courts. The following year, he knew what was needed, tried out for the team, and made it. That year that team went on to be national champions.

None of that would have happened had he not first gotten into the temple of his desire—the physical, mental, emotional, and spiritual space in which the thing he wanted existed. Because he wanted to be on that team, he needed to be in the space where the people who made up and supported that team were.

If your desire is to launch a clothing line, then you should make moves to be as close as possible to that dream until you catch it, or it catches you. If you must start out as a janitor in a clothing store or a packer in a clothing warehouse, it does not matter. What matters is you spend as much time as possible moving toward your goal. If Irv had spent that summer going swimming four hours a day, chances are at the end of the summer he would have been a much better swimmer, but no closer to making that team.

Action Step

↑ Choose one thing you want to do in life. Then identify three people who are doing it and talk to at least one of them right away. Identify three places it is being done and get to at least one place as soon as possible. Spend ten minutes picturing yourself doing the thing you want to do.

Chapter 3

The pro has faith with wisdom.

This one is tricky because many people confuse the process with the end product, and they are not one and the same. The *end product* is winning the prize, whatever that prize may be—the spouse, the new child, the promotion, better health, overcoming addiction, finding a place of worship. The *process* is the steps you take to get there. Two words that look similar are *faith* and *stubbornness*.

I will illustrate the difference with a joke.

An elderly woman is in her house when it starts raining and a flood warning is issued. A man comes to her door with an extra raincoat and galoshes and says, "Mary, the rain is coming, but I brought you a raincoat, and if we start walking now, we can make it to the bus station and get out of here." Mary says, "Not to worry, I have faith that God will save me." Reluctantly the man treads off. As the water begins to rise a woman is passing in her jeep and sees Mary in the house. The woman says, "Ma'am, I have room in my jeep for you, but we have to leave before the water gets too high." Mary says, "Not to worry, I have faith that God will save me." The woman shrugs and drives away. Finally, Mary is sitting on her second-floor landing, when a man motors up to the house in a boat. "Ma'am, I have enough room. Climb aboard and I will motor you out of here." Mary says, "I have faith, God will save me." "Okay," the man says, and sputtered off.

Mary drowned. Once in heaven, Mary strode right up to God and asked, "God, why didn't you save me?" "My dear Mary," God thundered, "I sent you rain gear, a jeep, and a boat, what more did you want me to do?"

Where people botch this one is that a definition of *faith* is "firm belief in something for which there is no proof." A definition of *stubborn* is "unreasonably or perversely unyielding." The two are similar, but here is the key degree of difference: Have a firm belief that you will get the something you are aiming for even if the proof is not immediately apparent; but do not be unreasonably or perversely unyielding when you receive information that your process is not working.

For example, say you have faith that you are going to get a great deal on a sailboat, which you plan to use to sail around the world. You have faith, you know what the boat looks, and you see yourself at the helm. You go to a desert looking for that boat, and the first person you meet says, "I am looking for a boat as well." I am driving cross-country to visit several harbors to find one. He suggests you go look in the harbors as well. You tell that person, "I have faith I will find a boat here." You spend the next year looking for a boat in the desert, despite overwhelming evidence that there is no boat there. Because of your passion and charisma, you have convinced others, who have never seen a boat on the desert, to believe you that there was one to be found. After a month of scouring the desert, you and your followers rejoice, because coming toward you is a pickup pulling a shiny, new sailboat. The boat is exactly as you described it. You flag down the pickup, and it is the first person you met when you came to the desert. In tears, you ask, "Is that my boat?" He replies, "Absolutely not, it is my boat that I found and bought in the harbor, where I told you to look."

Both people had faith, both were willing to go far to find the object of their faith, but only one was willing to adjust his plan until it succeeded.

Action Step

↑ Evaluate something you have been working on that has not gotten you the desired result. Ask yourself, "Am I looking for a boat in the desert, or do I need to change my approach?" Not only ask yourself, but also find boat owners and ask them as well. If it is something you are on fire to do or have, do not give up on it, just make sure you are adjusting your course based on real-time feedback.

Chapter 4

The pro asks, "What can we do for each other?"

The poet John Donne wrote: "No man is an island entire of itself; every man is a piece of the continent, a part of the main." Whatever your chosen field of endeavor, it will not occur in a vacuum. It will occur first in your mind, but then in the reality that unfolds around you. Inevitably, your journey toward your goal will cause you to interact with others. The goal of each interaction is that your interaction leaves both of you better off than before you met.

In Steven Covey's book *7 Habits of Highly Effective People*, Habit 4 is to think win/win. "Win/win is a frame of mind and heart that constantly seeks mutual benefit in all human interactions."

"Aha!" you say. "That doesn't make sense. Pros want to win, and for them to win, someone has to lose." You are correct, in a game or contest the goal is to win. By both sides striving toward that goal, both sides leave the contest better off than when they entered it. To think that you will always come in first place in everything you do is a leaky boat in deep waters. If you aim for first place, you will not only push yourself to do the best you can do, but also you will cause whomever is also vying for first place to push back as hard as they can. No matter who wins, you both leave the interaction having done your best.

Headed into the final stretch of the 2012 presidential election, Mitt Romney said this about his campaign team: "I feel we have put it all on the field. We left nothing in the locker room, we fought to the very end. And I think that's why we will be successful." Barack Obama went on to win that election, but the efforts of both men inexorably vying for a single goal took them to heights neither had achieved prior to that contest.

Living like a pro does not mean you will always get everything you want whenever you want it. It means even if you do not get exactly what you want, you can in your heart of hearts say, "I feel I have put it all on the field. I left nothing in the locker room, I fought to the very end." The shots Michael Jordan missed as well as the games he lost were as much a part of making him great as the shots he made and the games he won. Keep on shooting for greatness.

Action Step

↑ Play a game with friends, family, or associates, and not only play to win, but also encourage them to do the same. As iron sharpens iron, better opponents will help you become a better player.

Chapter 5

The pro is willing to launch.

You cannot steer a parked car, but you should have an idea where you are headed before you start driving. Look at a map, program your GPS, talk with others, and make plans for your trip, but get started as quickly as possible. If you want to play the piano, take lessons, talk to others, listen to great pianist play, but as quickly as possible start playing and practicing. Even when successful people do not make the right decisions, they know how to make their decisions right. They launch, receive feedback, and then correct their course of action as needed.

Author and speaker Brian Tracy says one thing that distinguishes successful people from unsuccessful people is the willingness to launch without any guarantee of success. This is not to say you should not plan nor have great plans. This is to avoid falling into the abyss of *someday*. *Someday* is an illusion. You should have a goal in mind before making a move—or else you have no idea what you are moving toward. There is a lot of good to be gained by training, but experience is the best training. The problem with not starting is all your experience is theoretical and may or may not survive its first contact with reality. Start small but start right away gaining your experience in your chosen field of endeavor. If you want to learn how to invest in stocks, for example, there are accounts that will let you start with as little as $10. If you start today, then a year from now you will have a year's experience of real-time investing. If you only study stocks, but do not invest, you will have a year's worth of planning that has never been tested. The best results come from study *and* application rather than study *or* application.

Action Step

↑ Find a task you have been putting off learning. Learn and apply one step in that task today.

Chapter 6

The pro is propelled by failure.

Remember, "If you want something you've never had. You must be willing to do something you've never done." The fact that you have never done something before increases the likelihood that you may fail at some of your early attempts.

Once when Irv was celebrating his birthday with his family and a couple of close friends. One of the friends told him about one of her family's traditions. The tradition was that since it was his birthday, he could ask others a question that helped them express how they felt about him. HIs question was, "What fond memory do you have of me and why?" His eldest son Jordan's memory was when he began teaching him how to shoot a basketball. Jordan said he remembered his first shot was an airball, but the airball did not define him. It drove him to keep trying until he improved his technique in practice and ultimately became a better shooter.

There are no 100% shooters in the game of basketball. The legendary Michael Jordan said, "I've missed more than 9,000 shots in my career. I've lost almost 300 games. Twenty-six times I've been trusted to take the game-winning shot and missed." Yet he is in history as one of the greatest professional basketball players of all times. In this life you will miss some shots but keep on shooting until you score.

Missing his first shot did not define him, it prepared him, and every missed shot since then is an opportunity to improve.

Action Step

↑ Choose a physical activity that you are not good at; only one activity, like throwing a baseball, swinging a golf club, jumping rope. Try doing it, and then find a coach, a video, a book, or someone else who knows how to do it and repeat it twenty-five times allowing each failure to prepare you to do better the next time.

Chapter 7

The pro focuses on the present solutions.

A while back my son Josh was reading this tongue-in-cheek self-help book *How to Be Miserable*. One chapter is titled, "Rehearse Your Regrettable Past." In it, the author writes: "The simplest strategy is to focus on the negative, replaying your distressing clips repeatedly. Inventory your losses. Remember past injuries. Recall the times you felt bereft, alone, alienated, terrified, and despondent. Include examples of random, uncontrollable fate knocking you about like a helpless pinball." This is not healthy nor helpful for you nor those around you. Keep any lessons you learned from those events but leave the events behind.

In life, mistakes are inevitable. Realize that whatever the mistake, no matter how big, replaying it over and over in your mind will not change it. It is a lot like having a thorn stuck in the palm of your hand. Instead of pulling it out and letting the hand heal, you clench your fist and hold on tighter to the thorn. For every second you do that, you are not only allowing the same thorn to keep hurting you, but you are also hindering the healing process as well as other new and wonderful things you could be doing with that hand.

Listen, in the course of my life I have made some mistakes that caused great loss and pain to myself and others. One decision had fatal consequences, while others lost me a lot of money. As sure as God sits high and looks low, I would change them if I could, but I cannot. For safety and sanity's sake, I had to unclench my fist and pull out the thorn and put my hand to good work in this present moment.

I want to emphasize here that if you make a mistake, especially one that causes someone else pain or loss, own and acknowledge the mistake. (We cover this in another chapter.) Go to that person and make direct amends wherever possible, except when doing so would cause harm to them or others. Once you have done that, let go of the hurt and live in the now.

Action Step

↑ Hand write a bad decision you made on a piece of paper. Then find someplace safe where you can set it on fire. Burn it and be done with it. By the way, I did this immediately after writing it. If you believe in a higher power (I believe in God), confess your mistake, and ask forgiveness. Find one other person you trust to keep your confidence and admit that mistake to that person. Now, whenever that mistake comes to mind, immediately do something positive in the present moment.

Chapter 8

The pro seeks criticism and feedback.

Three people helped me learn this lesson. The first was Dr. Thomas Kenneth Pinder. Kenneth was a police officer but was working on his doctoral degree in behavioral science. Despite working full-time, being a father, and going to school full-time, he still found time to mentor me. He embodied, "If you want something done, ask a busy person." Kenneth was working on an assignment for his doctoral thesis and asked me to review it and tell him what I thought. This was profound to me because prior to that, I had always considered criticism as hurtful and avoided it. It never occurred to me to seek out criticism to get better at something. Some of that came from the fact that a lot of the criticism I received came in the form a teasing and taunting; but Kenneth's desire not only to seek out criticism but utilize the suggestions if they improved what he was doing was an extraordinary skill in his toolkit for life. He did get his doctorate, by the way.

The next was my brother Ronald, who taught me that even if you do not like how something is said, nor who said something about what you are doing; if what they are saying is valid, then use it. Ronald is a missionary and has traveled all around the world serving others.

The last one was my best friend and co-author, Irving. When I met Irv, he was fourteen, six-feet-four-inches tall, in the tenth grade, and already playing on the varsity basketball team in high school. Irving was one of the most "coachable" people I had ever met. He relentlessly looked for ways to get better. He sought out feedback from coaches, his mother, his teammates, or anyone who had his best interest at heart, and then implemented those suggestions to the best of his ability. Irving's team, the Carol City Chiefs, went on to win a national championship. Irving went on to make several all-star teams, play college basketball, play professional basketball, and ultimately become the talent scout for the Los Angeles Lakers.

When I was in the tenth grade, and got assignments, I rarely worked with others or sought out help learning things I did not understand. I did them as quickly as I could and rarely reviewed them. I did not ask anyone else to review them before turning them in. I was happy to be done. I avoided anyone that might offer any suggestion as to how I might improve the assignment if it involved re-doing or investing more time in the assignment. My grades and performance showed that, as I ended up failing 10th grade and having to go to summer school. In the 11th and 12th grades, I began using what I had learned from Kenneth and sought out criticism as to how I could get better. I went from failing to making the principal's honor roll.

By the time I made it to the police academy, I had the two additional skills I had learned from Ronald and Irving, which were: (1) it does not matter who says it or how they say it; if it is valid use it, and (2) seek out others you trust to show you ways you can improve, and then use those ways. Those two skills not only helped get me hired, but I also finished number one in physical fitness and number two in my class overall. One of my assignments on the force was hostage negotiator. The negotiators worked in lockstep with the special response team. At the end of every tactical event, we debriefed and acknowledged what was done right and what could have been done better.

Similarly, as a college and professional basketball player, every week, Irving, and his team reviewed the previous week's games to see what he and the team did good and where they needed to improve. If you want to get better at whatever you are doing, do not be afraid to regularly review your performance. Identify what you did right as well as wrong. Keep doing the rights, stop doing the wrongs.

Action Step

↑ Find one mentor or coach you can trust in an area you are either currently working in or desire to work in. Ask them to critique something you are working on. See if their suggestion causes you to see the problem or more importantly its solution in a different light. If so, implement the change right away. Routinely, review big projects for things that were done well and things that could be done better.

Chapter 9

The pro asks, "What needs doing?

When my sons were in elementary school, I tried to teach them initiative. I explained it is good to pick up your clothes. However, picking them up when you are asked is *obedience*, but picking them up without having to be told is *initiative*. It would make great copy if I were to tell you they both got the lesson; I would be fudging the facts. However, they did demonstrate initiative in other areas of their lives. In the eleventh grade, Jay decided he wanted to play lacrosse. He had never played before, but set himself to learning the rules, mastering his equipment, and never missing a practice. Josh went on to win a presidential scholarship to the University of Florida (Go Gators!) where he graduated with a degree in biology. The initiative part comes in the fact that because I neither played lacrosse nor studied science, I could not offer specific help in those areas. Nevertheless, both my sons thrived due in large part to their own initiative.

Action Step

↑ Take an inventory of your workspace and determine what can be eliminated. Then eliminate it.

↑ Look at your living space or your car. Find one thing that needs fixing and either fix it or get it fixed.

↑ Pay attention to something that a co-worker, friend, spouse, or associate does. Without being asked, do it for that person. It could be bringing them their favorite soft drink, helping them put on their coat, walking them to the car, or carrying a parcel for them.

Chapter 10

The pro starts before time.

In the movie *Drumline*, the band director played by Orlando Jones told his band members, "If you're early, you're on time, and if you're on time, you're late." I know many time-challenged people who chronically underestimate the time it will take to arrive somewhere. They do not factor in possible delays, the time it takes to get in the car or to the bus, the time it takes to get to the location after you are off the bus, out of the Uber, or park the car; the time it will take on the elevator; and the time it takes to put on their makeup, straighten their tie, or use the restroom before they go in.

This is less of a problem if you are the only one affected, but it can be a great problem for others who are waiting for and depending on you. If you tell someone you will be there at three o'clock, then be all the way there, not on the way there at three o'clock.

Action Step

↑ Choose an organization (church, work, club) that you are a part of, and at the next meeting arrive early and do something that was not asked but will add value to the group. It can be as simple as bringing doughnuts, filling the water jar, or organizing the chairs.

Chapter 11

The pro under promises and over delivers.

Positive thinking can only carry you so far, and oftentimes people promise a product or service that they have no history of delivering nor proof that they can deliver. A widely used illustration of this is the story of David promising King Saul that he could defeat Goliath. Armed with just a slingshot, a stone, and faith, the small shepherd was able to defeat the Philistine giant. From that person could extrapolate and think, "I have faith like David, so even though I have never done a particular thing, I can do it. I am going to make it to the pros, be a CEO, marry the man or woman of my dreams." Not so fast, take a closer look at David's history. Yes, he was a shepherd, but he had Samuel the prophet as his mentor, telling him he was chosen by God to be king. Next, he had defeated a bear and lion before he ever agreed to step into the ring with Goliath. Then, even though he fell the giant with one stone, he brought five to the fight. Finally, after Goliath fell, he made sure Goliath stayed down. Before you put your neck, resources, or reputation on the line—or worse, someone else's neck, resources, or reputation on the line—ask yourself:

(1) Do I have a good mentor or coach?

(2) Do I have evidence that my faith has worked for me in other situations?

(3) Do I have a plan in case something goes wrong?

(4) When it succeeds, how will I solidify or anchor that success?

None of these questions mean you lack faith. My friends who are pilots all tell me they conduct pre-flight checks before taking off. That has nothing to do with faith and everything to do with common sense. Do not promise something based on blind faith that it will happen. Prepare, practice, and prove to yourself you can do it. Then you will be able to *under promise* and *over deliver*.

Action Step

↑ Pick one small assignment in the next week. Answer the four questions in the chapter. It can be as simple as putting up a shelf in the bathroom or as complicated as teaching your teenage child how to drive. Then under promise and over deliver.

Chapter 12

The pro can admit being wrong.

One year, my son Joshua, who was in college at the time, told me about a book a professor suggested he read. The book was *Being Wrong: Adventures in the Margin of Error* by Kathryn Schultz. "The book is an illuminating exploration of what it means to be in error, and why homo sapiens tend to tacitly assume (or loudly insist) that they are right about most everything." One of the opening quotes in that book is from the French playwright Molière, who said, "It infuriates me to be wrong when I know I'm right."

I have read the book twice and listened to the audiobook two more times. The chief lesson I took away from the book is the reluctance of people to simply say and mean, "I was wrong," and rarer still, "Please forgive me." Being wrong is such a challenge because being right feels great. Who does not like the sweet taste of the words, "I told you so"?

>Wife: I told you to turn left.

>Husband: I told you not to wear that dress.

>Father: I told you not to go.

>Mother: I told you he was no good.

Sister: I told you he would break your heart.

Brother: I told you not to try out for the team.

You could run this list *ad nauseum*. The eroticism of "I told you so" is that not only was I right, but you were wrong. Once the husband makes the wrong turn and causes him and his wife to be late to the wedding, that event is memorialized and available for recycling. "Remember when I told you to take the left turn and you went right and we were late for the wedding?" It is the sweetness of "I was right" that makes "I was wrong" taste so bitter.

Consequently, "I was right" comes with a double shot of espresso, while "I was wrong" gets watered down. Instead of "I was wrong," we get:

Wife: I don't care if we are early, you should have turned left.

Husband: Those people were just being polite when they complimented you on your dress.

Father: Even though you got the job, you were just lucky; you still should not have gone.

Mother: I don't care if he helped you pass chemistry; he wants something from you.

Sister: Even though you have been married twenty-five years and have four children, he is still going to break your heart one day.

Brother: So, what, you made the team, but I bet the coach won't play you.

The greatest shortfall of not admitting you are wrong is that you cannot fix what you do not own. If you do not own a mistake, it is not yours to fix. The chapter on criticism and feedback deals with this as well. Many times, when you care for others, you want to give them good advice. Sometimes, your best advice is wrong, because we are not perfect and cannot see all the possibilities of a decision. Often something looks clear and compelling based on the information you have, but one new piece of information can turn the situation on its ear. You were sure you left your keys on the table and someone moved them. After fifteen minutes of fussing and frustration, you snatch up your jacket only to hear the keys jingle in the pocket.

The wrong lesson to take away here is

because you can be wrong, do as little as possible to minimize the chances of making a mistake. That path leads mediocrity not greatness. The right lesson is to accept the imperfection of perception, make the best decisions possible, but be willing to accept when new information proves you wrong. I was watching a news reporter interview a politician once, and the reporter criticized the politician for changing her position on an issue. The politician responded, "That is what I do when I get new information. What do you do?" One word that will help immensely in this area is *maybe*. If you give yourself the wiggle room that exists between *maybe* I am wrong or *maybe* I am right, then neither position is absolute, and both allow for new information to change your view.

Laurick Ingram

Action Step

↑ The next time you are wrong, simply say, "I was wrong, please forgive me."

Chapter 13

The pro thinks action is more important than ambition.

Sean Hampton, American actor, director, and producer, said, "A dream without ambition is like a car without gas . . . you're not going anywhere." *Ambition*, that is, "a particular goal or aim: something that a person hopes to do or achieve," is important, but it is only an ingredient of success, not success itself. A delicious chocolate cake consists of eggs, flour, sugar or sugar substitute, and other ingredients mixed together then baked for the proper length of time.

Ambition, the chief ingredient in *desire* is critical to success, but without action it is no more than a clanging cymbal making noise and signifying nothing. There is a gentleman that was quite brilliant in many ways and had the ambition to produce concerts. He began throwing parties, which were well attended, and then finally launched and threw a full-blown concert with an A-list performer, which lost him a huge chunk of money. Just having the ambition was not enough. In fact, our example gentleman's ambition never wavered, and for twenty years after the failed concert, he continuously shared his grand ideas and plans with anyone who would listen. None of the lofty plans ever succeeded. He ended up losing his marriage, his home, and the one or two jobs he was able to land after the concert failure. Today you can see him on public transportation. He is usually unkept and is evasive about where he is living or how he is getting by. Although he has no visible means of support, he always has some grand plan that is going to make him a wealthy celebrity. Rich in ambition, poor in action. However great your ambition may be, without action, it is smoke and mirrors.

Action Step

↑ Think about a goal that is important to you. Can you objectively measure an action you are taking that is moving you toward that goal? If it is getting a degree, are you taking at least one class? If it is finding a mate, are you dating or meeting people? If it is joining a church, are you visiting churches? Whatever your ambition, as quickly as you can, get it off the drawing board of your mind and into the real world.

Chapter 14

The pro faces fear.

"One acronym for *FEAR* is fear everything and run, while another is face everything and rise. Change can be scary and the greater the change, the scarier it can be. Elevating your efforts to achieve greater heights, by its very nature can cause trepidation. You are drifting away from the shore into deeper water. Many times, the thing you desire most—writing a best seller, losing twenty pounds, rock climbing, white water rafting, getting your degree, or getting a promotion—is not where you currently are. If it is not where you are and you want it, you must go where it is. Any journey, no matter how well mapped out, comes with unknowns. The way to handle this is to define your goal, set your course, and then infuse your thinking with an unswerving belief that whatever happens, unexpected or not, you will handle it and soldier on.

Take a lesson from the U.S. Marines playbook: "Marines are trained to improvise, adapt, and overcome any obstacle in whatever situation they are needed. They have the willingness to engage and the determination to defeat the enemy until victory is seized."

Sometimes we are our own greatest enemy and must conquer ourselves and our fears before we can go forward.

Action Step

↑ We want to emphasize this step is not a license to be reckless—to jump from a third-floor balcony into a pool. We are not dealing with rational fears, but rather irrational fears. If you want to skydive, you need the right attitude, gear, and training. If you want to speak before large audiences, the same applies. Before you decide to face your fear, decide what gear, how much training, and what skills are required to do it successfully. Then be about the business of putting those things in place. If you can do that successfully, you are ready for the attempt. If you cannot do those things, maybe the goal is not worth the work it takes to achieve it.

Chapter 15

The pro says, "I'm hurting, but I can play."

In the movie *GI Jane*, Demi Moore plays a female candidate for the Navy SEALs, and Viggo Mortensen plays the master chief who is training her. In one scene he has a conversation with her:

Master Chief John Urgayle: Pain is your friend, your ally, it will tell you when you are seriously injured, it will keep you awake and angry, and remind you to finish the job and get the hell home. But you know the best thing about pain?

Lt. Jordan O'Neil: Don't know!

Master Chief John Urgayle: It lets you know you're not dead yet!

When you begin to push yourself to new limits it might be painful. For a muscle to grow or get stronger, for a brain to grow or get wiser, some time, somewhere, there will be pain.

There was a recovering alcoholic named Bill with only a few days sober when a friend of his was murdered. He went to Bob, an older guy who had been sober for more than thirty years, and asked Bob, "What do I do?" Bob said, "You get to hurt, and you don't pick up a drink." Prior to that, whenever bad things happened, Bill could drown the pain in booze, but once the booze was gone, he had to go through the pain in order to grow through the pain.

Life may hurt you physically, emotionally, mentally, spiritually, or any combination thereof. Take a tick to acknowledge life hurt you. There is no shame in grieving. Do not, however, allow yourself to wallow in that pain. Because you are in pain, you know you are still here, and if you are still here, there are things yet to be done. However great the injury, believing you can heal is the first step toward healing. "Ah," you say, "my beautiful sweet child died before he was fifteen," or "I lost my legs in a crash," or "I have terminal cancer."

There was a pastor whose fifteen-year-old son died from an illness. A few years later she traveled to an African orphanage and adopted another child, who she is caring for. A police officer lost both his legs in a motorcycle crash now works out five times a week and is still on the job. A missionary diagnosed with terminal cancer three years ago has traveled to six countries, ministered to over a thousand people, and still makes it to church on a regular basis.

Do you think any of them have known pain in their lives? Whether your goal is to live life like a pro or not, pain will come. Accept it, acknowledge it, and press on.

Action Step

↑ The next time you are hurting, tell yourself, "I am hurting because I am here. The only people not hurting are those who are not here. I acknowledge my pain, but I will press on toward the prize that awaits me and the good I can do for others."

Chapter 16

The pro says, "I practice even when I don't feel like it."

There is a scene in the movie *Star Trek VI: The Undiscovered Country*, where Commander Spock and Captain Kirk set a trap to find a traitor on their spaceship. The traitor turns out to be Spock's mentee, Lieutenant Valeris. When she tells Spock, she did not want to hurt him, he replies, "What you want is irrelevant, what you have chosen is at hand." How you practice affects how you perform. The better you practice, the better you perform. There will be many days that you will not feel like practicing. Car accidents, bruises and strains, relationship issues, melancholy moments, crises of faith, or plain old laziness will happen. The more you let those things keep you from practicing, the more your performance will suffer.

Both my sons won scholarships (one for academics, the other for music) to a college prep school. They both graduated as National Merit Scholars. When they went off to college, I told them that more than likely they would be able to do the academic work required by their courses, but what they would have to master was the art of getting up, going, and doing even when they did not feel like it. College distractions include girls, boys, parties, spring break, games, social media, and more. There is a time and place for all those things, but you can overdo any of them to the point of detraction from your studies. My sons' abilities to set aside those things, show up to their classes, and do the work required would make or break them. It made them and they both graduated.

Action Step

↑ If you have a job interview, a speech, a sermon, an exam, a line dance group, a ski trip, or some other event, practice the way you want to perform, no excuses.

Chapter 17

The pro believes it matters whether I win or lose, and how I play the game.

In the blockbuster movie *Pitch Perfect*, two of the Bellas, Alice and Audrey, are speaking before a performance. The exchange goes:

> Alice: …I can't believe the Bellas are being passed on to you two slut bags after we graduate. [To Aubrey] Just don't eff up your solo.
>
> Aubrey: I won't disappoint you. My dad always says, "If you're not here to win, get the hell out of Kuwait."

The statement referred to the Gulf War, which began when Iraq invaded Kuwait and the U.S. intervened. The reasons and complexities of war go well beyond the scope of this book, but if you are a soldier inserted into a war zone, you better be there to win.

If you have decided something is important to you, becoming a pastor, passing the CPA exam, graduating high school, making the lacrosse team, or getting an A in chemistry, begin with an expectation of succeeding. If succeeding is not important, then maybe your goals are not the right goals. We get it, the more you want something, the greater the disappointment if you do not get it, but just because you did not get it does not mean wanting it was wrong. By going for the gold, you can walk away knowing you left it all on the field. You should not like losing, but in every loss, there is a lesson. It is a double tragedy to lose and not get the lesson.

Hunter S. Thompson said, "Life should not be a journey to the grave with the intention of arriving safely in a pretty and well-preserved body, but rather to skid in broadside in a cloud of smoke, thoroughly used up, totally worn out, and loudly proclaiming, 'Wow! What a ride!'" And that is how you should go after your important goals.

Action Step

↑ Think about one thing you want to do or accomplish. Picture in your mind what winning will look like and experience it with as many of your senses as possible. The taste, touch, sight, smell, and sound of it. The extra money, the accolades, the sense of satisfaction. Create a vivid, clear picture in your mind, and then GO! FOR! IT!

Chapter 18

The pro has the audacity to believe in the yet unseen.

The Scottish philosopher Thomas Carlyle said, "Go as far as you can see; when you get there, you'll be able to see farther." December 2011, I got the idea to deliver one thousand pairs of sneakers to the children of Haiti. An earthquake had devastated Haiti in 2010, and the small country was still recovering. I told Irv about it, and he said, "I'm in." And so, began the project:

Sneakers for Haiti. Understand that I only spoke about thirty words of Creole and had never been to Haiti. I was not supported by a charitable foundation and Haitian friends I had did not have any current connections in the small country. That being said, Irv and I launched. The next person to sign on was my pastor, Bishop Curry, who gave us airtime on the radio as well as a big donation. A good friend and financial advisor Mike Richter immediately donated a large sum to purchase sneakers. Scott Howard, another NBA scout that was friends with Irv, gave money. A talk show host on a Haitian owned radio station heard us on WMBM, our church's radio station and asked to interview us. A woman named Yveline Achille, whom we had never met heard the interview, phoned the station, and said God told her to help us. She explained that she was not a part of an organization but had on her own decided to help some children in a village outside of Port au Prince.

It took five months, but we raised 1,200 pairs of sneakers. Then there was the matter of boxing them and shipping them. At that time, I did not know that many of the things shipped to Haiti get held up in customs for months. I flew to Haiti ahead of Irv. There was a mix-up, and Yveline, who was supposed to meet me at the airport, was not there. My cell phone was not working, because I had planned to get a local one there. On the plane ride over, I had met a man named Aldi Castor. He was a Haitian physician that volunteered to go to Haiti and teach. I explained to him what I was doing, and he said I could share his taxi, and he would drop me at my hotel.

The hotel turned out to be where military personnel stationed to assist with disaster relief were staying. I got to spend time with some of heroic armed forces members. The following day, Irv and his wife, Natasha, arrived. Yveline met us at the hotel and acted as our translator the entire trip. Also, her cousin, who was someone big in Haitian government, loaned us a Toyota SUV and provided us with a driver.

I will not go into details about how we got the shoes through customs, as I do not want to get anyone in trouble, but I will say it was challenging. I will also say without our angel Yveline, it would have been impossible. We had to make three deliveries of the sneakers, which took the entire day. We ended our day in the village outside of Port au Prince, with the children Yve had "adopted." This was the only sad part here. Yve had told us how many children were there. We brought more sneakers than we needed figuring we would have extras, but apparently the word had spread that we were coming, and children had come from other villages. We had more children than shoes. I had Yve explain to them how sorry I was, and I promised that for Christmas I would make sure they all got gifts. That Christmas, with Yve's help my wife and I bought and shipped more than enough gifts for all the children in the village.

While I was there and even after I returned, I heard all sorts of reasons why it should not have worked and what a risk we had taken. People told me that a Florida highway patrolman in Haiti visiting his ailing wife was gunned down a short time after we had left. Additionally, many other people had shipped things to Haiti and never seen those things again.

All we can say is that because we had the audacity to act on the *"yet unseen,"* we were able to do the *"it is done."*

Action Step

↑ Start small but take one idea and grow it from the "*not yet seen*" to the "*it is done.*"

Chapter 19

The pro faults self when something is not working.

It is axiomatic that in human interactions the person you have the most control over is yourself. The Big Book of Alcoholic Anonymous outlines a twelve-step strategy for living that helps people recover from the disease of alcoholism. Step Four is "took a fearless and searching moral inventory of ourselves." This involves making a list of persons you harmed and being willing to make amends to them. The book explains, "Putting out of our minds the wrongs others had done, we resolutely looked for our own mistakes. Where had we been selfish, dishonest, self-seeking, and frightened? Though a situation had not been entirely our fault, we tried to disregard the other person entirely . . . The inventory was ours, not the other man's. When we saw our faults, we listed them. We placed them before us in black and white. We admitted our wrongs honestly and were willing to set these matters straight."

We are sure that if you have spent any time on this earth aware of your surroundings, there have been instances where "people done you wrong." The challenge here is that sometimes they saw their actions as justified or provoked. Other times they did not see them at all. And still other times, they knew they were wrong and intended to do it. Your aim is to get better, whether they change or not, because maybe they will never change. If you base your growth and change on whether someone else grows and changes, you are surrendering your ability and responsibility to improve your own life to forces outside of your control.

One area this is seen a lot is in romantic relationships. Usually, breakups come with a lot of hurt, by one or both. Rarely is one partner all right and the other all wrong. There are usually rights and wrongs on both sides, even if the wrong was "you should have left them long ago." Whatever you should or should not have done, is the part of the relationship you had the greatest control over. Focus on what *you* could have done better. If you can do so without hurting anyone, apologize and make amends for it. Even if you cannot make amends, for example, if the person died, acknowledge the mistakes, and do your best not to carry them into your next relationship.

Action Step

↑ Think about someone you are angry at or who hurt you. Set aside what they did and look for anything you did that was wrong. If possible, and if you can do it without injury to them or others, apologize for what you did and make amends.

Chapter 20

The pro wants to be coached.

A business professor at the University of Miami, said sometimes motivating employees requires the management principle of AKITA. What, you ask, is AKITA? a kick in the ass. He asserted that some employees are not self-starters and set a goal to do the minimum acceptable amount of work required to not to get fired. Often, AKITA is the only way to get better and more from an employee with this type of mind-set.

There was a police detective who used to say if he showed up for work, he had earned his pay. If he chose to do more once he got there, that was more than he owed. If anyone needed AKITA, it was that detective. He would sit at his desk, watching who knows what on the computer, and when the supervisor would walk by, he would ask, "Do you need anything?" In his mind, if the supervisor did not ask for anything, it was not his fault. Despite his assignment being clearly spelled out in the department's general orders, he simply believed all that was owed was what was asked. If nothing was specifically asked of him, his being there was fulfilling his duties. He was the embodiment of someone in need of coaxing with AKITA. His supervisor was ecstatic when he was transferred.

The young detective that took his place was wound up tighter than the Energizer Bunny. He worked, overworked, and worked some more. He was constantly in the supervisor's office, asking to be coached on the different dimensions of his job. Long after he left the assignment, he continued rising in his career and eventually was the lead on one of the department's biggest investigations. Clearly, the former was an amateur and the latter a pro.

Think long and hard before you pursue something. If you have decided the something you are pursuing is worthwhile, then do not wait for

AKITA; set a fire under your own butt and pursue it with all the energy and focus you can muster and sustain.

Action Step

↑ "If you're playing a poker game and you look around the table and can't tell who the sucker is, it's you." Take a cold hard look at what you are doing and not doing and make sure you're not the one who needs AKITA.

Chapter 21

The pro pivots when something is not working.

In his book *The Lean Startup*, Eric Ries describes how the *build-measure-learn loop* helps businesses decide how to proceed. He defines it this way: "The fundamental activity of a startup is to turn ideas into products, measure how customers respond, then learn whether to pivot or persevere." He explains in any startup there are two leap-of-faith assumptions. The first is the *value hypothesis*—your idea, widget, service is something that people will pay for; and the second is the *growth hypothesis*—once the idea, widget, or service is offered, more people will want to use it and be willing to pay for it.

The build-measure-learn loop tests this as quickly as possible, because if you cannot prove the first hypothesis—the thing has value and someone is willing to pay for—producing more of it will not make a difference; hence, the decision to pivot or persevere.

For us, the build-measure-learn loop works in other aspects of life besides business, and the pivot is a two-pronged possibility. You can pivot toward either a new product or a new process. For example, suppose your native language is English.

You plan to take a trip to Barcelona, Spain in a year. By then you want to be able to speak Spanish fluently. You enroll in an online course, and after thirty days, you cannot so much as order a *café con leche*, the online course is not working, and you need to try a different course or hire a tutor. In this case you pivot from the process you are using to a different process, until you find the one that gets you the best results. If none of them get you better results, you now must decide if you want to pivot away from the product—your ability to speak Spanish fluently. Instead of speaking Spanish fluently, your goal is to find and hire a translator that is fluent in both English and Spanish. You can still get to Barcelona and will be able to communicate effectively with the Spanish speakers, but your build-measure-learn loop caused to you find a different way to achieve that goal.

Action Step

↑ Pick one idea you have been nursing recently. Measure your results and decide if it is time to pivot or persevere?

Chapter 22

The pro failed six times but succeed the seventh time.

I got an "F" in physical education in the tenth grade at Miami Springs. That semester we were doing tumbling, and one of the skills was doing a handspring. This meant taking two steps, locking out your arms, pitching your weight forward on your palms, launching your legs up and over, and landing on your feet. If you did not launch with enough spring, you would either not get your feet up in the air, or worse, land flat on your back on the mat. The latter was what I did. After a few failed attempts I was too afraid to try any more, and I sat it out. One of my classmates—I cannot remember his name, but he was roughly my age, height, and weight—fell as many times as I did, but every time he landed flat on his back, he got up, got back in line, a tried it again. Before the week was out, he was doing handsprings and I got an F.

Two years later in alone in my front yard at the house on 65th Street, I decided I would learn how to do a handspring. Surprise, surprise, my first attempts landed me flat on my back, but this time I kept at it, ignoring the failed attempts and pain. I do not remember how many attempts I made; all I remember is the elation I felt when I tried one last time and finally did it.

I learned three important lessons that day: (1) the difference between success and failure, lies in one attempt more than the other; (2) even though it took me two years to learn what my classmate learned in one week, it is better to learn something late rather than not at all; and (3) to this day, the number of times I failed do not matter to me; what mattered was that I did a handspring.

Action Step

↑ This week find something you want to improve on or have been wanting to learn but gave up. Try it one more time and see what happens.

Chapter 23

The pro acts based on vision.

A president of a railroad visited one of his depots. He ran into a man who had begun working for the railroad around the same time as he did. The man said, "Years ago you and I were laying track together. Now I am still laying tracks and you're a big shot." Smiling, the president replied, "You were laying tracks; I was building a railroad company." The secret sauce in many success stories is when people were given the same assignment, but one had sight while the other had vision.

I knew four waiters. Waiter One's goal was only interested in making the most tips, and he flitted from restaurant to restaurant until last I heard he was fired. Waiter Two wanted to give diners a five-star experience when they came in. She is still at the same restaurant and is in great demand by people who have had the pleasure of being served by her. Waiter Three did not want to go to college and wanted to learn as much as he could about the restaurant business. He has held several jobs in the current restaurant where he works and is a troubleshooter that is helping that chain launch several franchises. Waiter Four was working his way through college and graduated with a degree in marketing and is pursuing his dream career in the music industry.

Three years ago, had you come into the restaurant, you would have seen four people waiting tables. What you would not have seen is the vision each held in their head and heart. There is a saying a woman used to have on her voice message. It went, "Anyone can count how many seeds are in an apple, but only God can count how apples will grow from a seed." Whatever you are doing today and wherever you are doing it, write a vision, make it plain, and run with it. Live life like a pro, and you can be and should be the MVP of your life.

Action Step

↑ Take a moment to see something you are doing at work or at home. Now, write a vision for something great to come from that.

Chapter 24

The pro falls going forward.

Victor Kiam, former owner of the New England Patriots, said, "Even if you fall on your face, you're still moving forward." Nothing in this book guarantees success but doing nothing this book suggests increases your chances of failure. As you apply these principles to your life, there are going to be fits, fumbles, and falls. It would be great if all of life's challenges had clear-cut right or wrong answers, but the Grand Architect of this world chose not to make it so. I have known great successes and grand failures. Many times, when I failed, I was trying just as hard as when we succeeded. I have had my heart broken and I am sure I have broken some hearts. I have made money and lost money. I have zagged left when I should have zigged right, gone up when I should have gone down. I have as many successes in my book of life as I have failures. As long as I fell going forward, I knew I was closer to the object of my desire.

It would be great if I could tell you do this thing three times or that thing seven times and I guarantee you will succeed, but I am not a soothsayer. I am just someone willing to bring my best game onto the playing field life as early and often as I can. Since failures and mistakes are inevitable, it is best to get the most use out of them. Fail because you had the audacity to attempt something great. Every great thing you attempt will not work, but sometimes the one great thing that does can change the course of your life.

On Irv's journey to the NBA, there were many tryouts, missed shots, failed camps, and lost scrimmages. Every failure brought him closer to his dream until the LA Lakers signed him. That was his vision. Know your vision and set a fire in your soul that will burn towards it.

Action Step

↑ Sit still for ten minutes and recall something you failed at. If you still want it, identify what you can do better and do it again.

Chapter 25

The pro learns from past mistakes.

    I recognize that some ideas presented here are reiterations of concepts already covered; but these concepts are worth emphasizing. You cannot unscramble eggs, un-ring a bell, nor undo one second of the past. No matter how beautiful or dreadful it was, whatever you did in the past is past. What you can do in the present is acknowledge where you went wrong, ask forgiveness of anyone you hurt, forgive yourself, and make amendments wherever possible except when to do so would injure them or others. You can also replay your victories, study what you did right, and continue forward with those "did-right" abilities in your life skills toolkit.

There is cliché in police work: "Big cases, big problems; little cases, little problems; no cases, no problems." It was usually said by lazy detectives who justified their lack of productivity by pointing to the problems hardworking detectives came up against by choosing to work complex cases. A similar adage outside of criminal investigations was, "A way not to make mistakes is do not try anything new." Both remarks sound pithy, but don't hold water.

The hole in the bottom of the police saying is that the cases involve real victims. Although doing nothing may simplify the officer's life, it leaves the victim swinging in the wind. No problems for the cop means big problems for the victims. The leak in the second one is that many a mistake was made by standing still. Life and the world around us are in a constant state of flux. We inhale, we exhale; we sit, we stand; we are born, we live, we die. To do little or nothing in the precious fleeting minutes of life we are given is a great mistake. Life moves inexorably forward, and even if you made it a point to avoid change as much as you could, the world around you are changing every day. You can either run with it or be run over by it. Another consideration for avoiding learning and changing is that people who do avoid it can afford to do so because they are comfortable in their present circumstance. Eugene and Sarah are an elderly couple whose adult daughter, Deborah, is in the advanced stages of multiple sclerosis. They look for and are willing to change at the speed of light if it means the possibility of extending the length and quality of Deborah's life. Their burning need fuels their engine of change. If your child is healthy, you do not suffer from the same fierce urgency of now to find a cure. If you did your willingness to grow and learn would be on fire.

Action Step

↑ Step out of your comfort zone and either start learning one new thing in the next twenty-four hours or learn a new way to do something you have been doing the same way for a while. Repeat the new way for a week and see what you learn from it. For example, change how you shave, where you wash your car, the route you take to work, the time (more or less) you spend with a family member; read a new book; or try a new food or the same food prepared differently.

Chapter 26

The pro knows how to use tools of opportunity.

During my 27 years as an officer, I learned the life-saving lesson of using *tools of opportunity* versus *tools of choice*. For example, we carried rope and full-sized spare tires in our trunks. Also, my equipment—belt, body armor, shoes, etc.—weighed twenty-two pounds. If I happened upon someone drowning, it would be great if I had the tools of choice, such as swim trunks, goggles, a snorkel, and a raft, but those things were not standard issue. If I jumped in the water with twenty-two extra pounds of weight trying to save someone, since I was not a Navy SEAL nor a triathlete, there was a good chance we would both drown. What I did have were tools of opportunity, namely a rope, and a tire that floated. I could shed as much equipment as I could, tie the tire to the rope, anchor the rope to something solid, and then go save the person. Although the latter takes a little longer, it has the best probability of success. Often, you will not have the tools of choice to tackle a task. Train yourself to look for and use tools of opportunity.

Action Step

↑ Think back to a time in your life that a tool of opportunity helped you succeed. Make a note of it, and then in the next problem you are confronted with identify three tools of opportunity that can help you and use one.

Chapter 27

The pro knows the difference in having a best friend and being best friends.

I was speaking to a group of young men ages seven to seventeen at my church. The group was called IMPACT, and the vision was to teach them that they could "impact the world, one soul at a time."

One of our deacons would bring a group from Miami-Dade Corrections Bootcamp. The program utilizes an inmate management system known as "*shock incarceration* and *regimented inmate discipline* in a paramilitary setting integrating academic, vocational, rehabilitative programs, the Thinking for a Change model, structured activities, and a wide array of services."

Participants consist of convicted offenders between the ages of fourteen and twenty-four, with those under eighteen having been adjudicated as adults and mandated to go into the program as part of their sentence. Participants receive general equivalency diploma (GED) preparation, vocational training, postsecondary education assistance, financial literacy, skills training, job placement, and volunteer opportunities. As part of the program, inmate visitation is considered a privilege and granted during graduation and family night.

One of the offenders was arrested and charged with possession of a firearm. He explained that he and his "best friend" were riding in a car and his best friend had a pistol with him. They got pulled over by the police and his "best friend" convinced him to say the gun was his. The best friend already had a criminal record and told him that because he did not have a record, the police would go easy on him. My pastor weighed in on that one and said something that stuck with me for years. "Does THE person you call your best friend always call you their best friend?" It is a profound distinction.

I grew up in Liberty City, and it would not

be inaccurate to say I was around some criminals. One of them sold drugs on 69th Street and 18th Avenue, and the other was an armed robber. Both men did prison time, and both cared deeply for me. Never once did either ask me to do anything wrong. In fact, both encouraged me to stay in school and do something good with my life. I think the young man from bootcamp I talked about earlier was confused when he talked about his best friend. A real best friend would not save himself at the expense of his friend.

Irving and I are best friends. He is the godfather to my children, and I to his. When my mother was in intensive care at Mt. Sinai Hospital, he slept on a couch in the waiting room while I sat vigil over her until the Lord called her home. He was traveling when his father died at home. I went to the house and helped carry the body out to be transported to the funeral home. When I got married, he was there. When he got married, I was there. He was there for the birth of both my sons, and I for the birth of his daughter, son, and twin sons. I was there when he signed his professional basketball contract with the Lakers, and he was there when I got hired as a police officer. For every hill and every valley that he or I have experienced, all we had to do was look right or look left and the other was there.

If you are blessed to have a best friend, be sure that you *are* a best friend. My best friend has helped me to live life like a pro, and I have helped him. We both hope the ideas put forth in this book will help build the champion in you.

Action Step

↑ Do something nice for your best friend today, even if it is just to tell him you love them.

Afterword

Thank you for sharing your precious time with me. I would enjoy keeping in contact with you. You can find me on us, Irving Thomas and Laurick Ingram, on social media. If you have enjoyed this book, please take a moment to write a review on Amazon Books. If there is something you would like to see changed, please contact us directly with your comments and we will get back to you.

God bless!

Acknowledgements

I thank
- God;
- My wife Kim and my sons Joshua and Jawanza;
- My seven brothers Sonny, Bobby, Kelsey, Ronald, Is, Nog, and Chuck;
- My three sisters Betty, Toy, and Thyl;
- My brother Ronald for showing me "faith with works, Sonny for being a father to me after daddy died; Bobby for showing me the value of study, and Toy for her unconditional love;
- My pastor Bishop Victor Curry, who looked at a rock on a vacant lot but saw the cathedral that exists their today;
- Da-Venya L Armstrong, Sam Grant and the team at Armstrong Creative Consulting, Inc. who got my first book from out of my head and into the world;
- Roderick Harvey, C.P.A., C.V.A, for all his support;
- My friends, my followers, my readers, and anyone I know who dares to live life like a pro.

About the Author

Laurick is addicted to success stories. Learning from or helping people develop their dreams into real-life victories winds his crank. Starting with his mother who gave birth to nine children (not counting three miscarriages) after marrying a man who already had two children. Although she never made it past the fifth grade, her children would go from living in the government housing projects to serving in the Navy, Army, Air Force, and Marines. All of them would earn high school diplomas, and five would graduate college. They would become an airline worker, a teacher, a PhD, a pastor, a mayor, a police chief, an accountant, a yacht design school graduate, an international missionary, an interior decorator, postal workers, a janitor, a police officer, and an author. Arimentha Ingram mothered like a pro.

Laurick is the founder of Give and Save 3-6-5, a company dedicated to teaching people how to add value to their lives and the lives of others. In addition to this book, he has written and published. the Easy Money Management Guide, the Easy Money Management Weekly Journal, and Student Loan Exit Plan. He believes people can grow their giving through faith and grow their faith through saving. The United Nations Association (Broward

Chapter) honored him for his efforts to eradicate poverty. He is a proud member of the 5000 Role Models of Excellence. He has been interviewed on radio and television and has been mentioned in more than one hundred journals and publications. Laurick lives in South Florida with his wife, Kim, and their two sons, Joshua and Jawanza.

THE END

www.ingramcontent.com/pod-product-compliance
Lightning Source LLC
LaVergne TN
LVHW051604070426
835507LV00021B/2767